CH

A DE MIS AÑOS PEORES

CHRONICLE OF MY WORST YEARS

CRÓNICA DE MIS AÑOS PEORES

Tino Villanueva

TRANSLATED BY JAMES HOGGARD

TRIQUARTERLY BOOKS
NORTHWESTERN UNIVERSITY PRESS

Evanston, Illinois

TriQuarterly Books
Northwestern University Press
Evanston, Illinois 60208-4210

Some of these translations, in slightly different form, first appeared in
RE: Arts & Letters, The Texas Observer, and *TriQuarterly.*

Crónica de mis años peores was first published 1987 in slightly different
form by Lalo Press, La Jolla, California. Copyright © 1987, 1994 by
Tino Villanueva. Translation and afterword copyright © 1994 by James
Hoggard. *Chronicle of My Worst Years/Crónica de mis años peores*
published 1994 by Northwestern University Press/TriQuarterly Books.
All rights reserved.

Printed in the United States of America

ISBN   0-8101-5009-3 cloth
       0-8101-5034-4 paper

Library of Congress Cataloging-in-Publication Data

Villanueva, Tino.
    Chronicle of my worst years = Crónica de mis años peores / Tino
Villaneuva ; translated by James Hoggard.
        p.   cm.
    "TriQuarterly books."
    ISBN 0-8101-5009-3 (alk. paper). — ISBN 0-8101-5034-4 (alk. paper
: pbk.)
    1. Mexican Americans—Poetry. I. Hoggard, James. II. Title.
III. Title: Crónica de mis años peores.
PQ7079.2.V47C47   1994
861—dc20   94-20485
                                                            CIP

The paper used in this publication meets the minimum requirements of
the American National Standard for Information Sciences—Permanence
of Paper for Printed Library Materials, ANSI Z39.48-1984.

Chronicle of my worst
years, I said
only what was mine,
I drank in the vile
sorcery of erosion
and baptized
my own life's story
with rubble.

"Having It Out with Myself"
J. M. Caballero Bonald

Crónica de mis años
peores, dije
lo que sólo era mío,
bebí del sortilegio
ruin de la erosión,
bauticé con escombros
la personal historia
de mi vida.

"Me pido cuentas"
J. M. Caballero Bonald

ÍNDICE

CONTENTS

CHRONICLE OF MY WORST YEARS

CRÓNICA DE MIS AÑOS PEORES

Clase de historia

Entrar era aspirar
la ilegítima razón de la clase,
ser sólo lo que estaba escrito.
Sentado en el mismo
predestinado sitio
me sentía, al fin, descolocado.
Miraba en torno mío
y nada alumbraba a mi favor.

Era cualquier mañana de otoño,
o primavera del 59, y ya estábamos
los de piel trigueña
sintiéndonos solos,
como si nadie abogara por nosotros,
porque entrar era arrostrar
los sofocantes resultados → sense of loss,
del conflicto: el estado   desespero
desde arriba
contra nosotros sin el arma
de algún resucitable dato
para esgrimir
contra los largos parlamentos
de aquel maestro

History Class

To enter was to breathe in
the illegitimate idea of the class:
only what was written was valid. → *It must be true*
Seated in the same
prescribed place
I felt myself, finally, dislocated.
I looked all around
and nothing was shining for me.

It was some morning in autumn,
or the spring of '59, and already we were
the wheat-colored people
who felt alien,
as if no one would intercede for us,
because to enter was to defy
the suffocating results
of the conflict: the state
from on high
against us with no weapon
of a retrievable date
to wield
against the long speeches
of that teacher

de sureña frente dura,
creador del sueño y jerarquías,
que repetía,
como si fuera su misión,
la historia lisiada de mi pueblo:

And beware of the Mexicans, when
they press you to hot coffee and
"tortillas." Put fresh caps on
your revolver, and see that your
"shooting-irons" are all in order,
for you will probably need them
before long. They are a great
deal more treacherous than Indians.

Entre los autores de la luz
no estuvo aquel corruptivo preceptor,
como tampoco fecundó
con fáciles sentencias
y cómplice actitud suprema
los cerebros listos de mi raza:

He will feed you on his best,
"señor" you, and "muchas gracias"
you, and bow to you like a French
dancing-master, and wind it all up

with the hard Southern mien,
creator of the dream and hierarchies,
who repeated,
as if it were his mission,
my people's crippled history:

And beware of the Mexicans, when
they press you to hot coffee and
"tortillas." Put fresh caps on
your revolver, and see that your
"shooting-irons" are all in order,
for you will probably need them
before long. They are a great
deal more treacherous than Indians.

That corrupt teacher was not
among the authors of the light,
nor did he help
the quick brains of my people grow
with his facile remarks
and snobbish attitude:

He will feed you on his best,
"señor" you, and "muchas gracias"
you, and bow to you like a French
dancing-master, and wind it all up

Imagine being in this position: racist, inflamatory

by slipping a knife under your
left shoulder-blade! And that's
one reason I hate them so.

Por no gritar mi urgente ira,
me encorvaba en el pupitre
como un cuerpo interrogante;
me imaginaba estar en otro estado,
sin embargo, fui cayendo
cada vez hacia el abismo espeso
de la humillación,
tema tenaz de mi tiempo.

El trato recibido en clase.

¿Quiénes éramos
si no unos niños
detenidos en la frontera perversa
del prejuicio, sin documentos
recios todavía
para llamarnos *libertad*?
Se me volvía loca la lengua.
Quería tan pronto saber
y decir algo para callar
el abecedario del poder,
levantarme y de un golpe
rajarle al contrincante las palabras
de obsesión, soltarle
los argumentos de nuestra fortaleza

by slipping a knife under your
left shoulder-blade! And that's
one reason I hate them so.

To keep from crying out the anger boiling up in me
I bent over my desk
like a human question mark;
I imagined myself in another state,
however, I was falling
each time toward humiliation's
dense abyss,
the persistent theme of my time.
Who were we
other than some kids
detained at the perverse border
of prejudice, still without
effective documents
to proclaim our *freedom*?
My tongue went crazy.
I wanted to know right away
and to say something to stop
the abecedarian of power,
to lift myself up and with one blow
split the enemy's
obsessive phrases, and let loose
arguments about our courage

y plantar, en medio de la clase,
el emblema de mi fe.
Pero todo era silencio,
obediencia a la infecta tinta
oscura de los textos,
y era muy temprano
en cualquier mañana de otoño,
o primavera del 59
para decir
lo que se tenía que decir.

*Todavía retienen
sus sentimientos*

Pero han pasado los años,
y los libros han cambiado
al compás del pueblo latidor,
porque sólo por un tiempo puede
un hombre llevar a cuestas
el fastidio
de quien se cree el vencedor.

Aquí mi vida cicatriza
porque soy el desertor,
el malvado impenitente que ha deshabitado
el salón de la demencia,
el insurrecto
despojado de los credos de la negación.

and plant, in the middle of class,
the badge of my faith.
But all was silence,
obedience to the infected
dark cast of the texts,
and it was too early
during that morning in autumn
or spring of '59
to say
what needed to be said.

But the years passed
and the books changed
to the beat of the people's rhythm,
because only for awhile
can a man carry on his back
the burden
of the one who thinks he's a conqueror.

Here my life scars over
because I'm the deserter,
the profane impenitent who quit
the crazy class,
the insurrectionist
stripped of the creeds of negation.

Sean, pues,
otras palabras las que triunfen
y no las de la infamia,
las del fraude cegador.

ends on a positive note

So let there be
other words that are triumphant
and not the ones of infamy,
those of the blinding fraud.

Empezando a saber

No sé qué me da por abrir
las puertas malditas del tiempo
y ver de nuevo el barrio
polvoriento entre el cascajo,
donde aprendí a ser menos de lo que era.
Seguramente porque me hice tal,
porque he llegado, para bien o para mal,
hasta esta orilla de mi vida,
y más porque el compás de mi memoria
es mi conducta,
pongo ahora la maciza rebelión de las palabras
al candor de este papel.

Cierro los ojos
y empiezo a saber la extensión de mi Nada,
vuelvo a sentir el mismo asco,
la insolvencia de entonces
cuando un terrón perdido en el olvido
era mi cuerpo,
desmoronándose con cada lluvia
de lenta negación:
Cuántas veces
        en lo hondo de la tarde
        me quedé sentado a ras de la tierra

Beginning to Know

I don't know what got me to open
time's damn doors
and see again
the dusty, gravelly barrio
where I learned to be less than I was.
Surely because I did something with myself,
because I've arrived, for better or worse,
at this stage of my life,
and even more because my guide
is the beat of my memory,
I now put the massive rebellion of words
on this paper's whiteness.

I close my eyes
and begin to know the extent of my Nothingness,
I return to feel the same loathing,
the inadequacy of that time
when lost in forgetfulness
my body was a clod
diminished by the rains
of slow negation:
Time and time again
    deep in the afternoon
    I stayed sitting on the ground

recargado en la morosa sombra de un nogal,
como esperando el advenimiento de una luz;
cuántas veces
    en el último reducto de la noche
    nadie me ungió de salvación, alzándome
    algún pedazo de verdad ante mis ojos;
cuántas veces
    no me rescataron de la invasión multiplicada
    de preguntas, pues nadie me explicó
    por qué mi casta no contaba,
    por qué nombrar las cosas
    a mi modo con mi lengua
    equivalía a traicionar
    los códigos sajones de pureza.
Y levantándome con la hombría de doce años
me sacudía el polvo de la ira,
harto de tener que resollar,
preguntándome cuál dictamen o decreto,
cuál fuerza abolidora deshacía mi sonrisa,
los juegos de trompos, canicas y *baseball*.

Alma ocupada fue la mía en los días gachos
de mi tiempo, en la recia cerrazón
de mis horas juveniles
que hoy se agolpan en mi frente.
Voy juntando mis años
en la contienda del presente,

slumped back in the deep shade of a pecan tree,
as if waiting for the coming of light;
time and time again
in the last redoubt of the night
no one hoisting some bit of truth before me
anointed me with salvation;
time and time again
they did not rescue me from the endless invasion
of questions, and no one explained to me
why people like mine did not count,
why naming things
in my own way with my own language
was equivalent to betraying
Saxon purity codes.
And rising with my twelve-year-old's courage
I brushed the dust of my rage away,
enough so I could breathe,
asking myself which judgment or decree,
which destructive power undid my smile,
my games: tops, marbles, baseball.

My soul was caught up with the meanness
of my time, with the harsh storm-threat
of my boyhood hours
that crowd my brain today.
Gathering the fragments of my ruin
at the base of all the borders

recogiendo los fragmentos de mi ruina
al pie de las unánimes fronteras
contra las cuales mis años indefensos
sin paz se desgastaron.
Le doy, por fin, sentido a lo perdido,
le pongo nombre al porvenir
porque hoy me pertenezco,
soy la fundación de lo que creo
y no de lo que fui.

Identidad??

my defenseless years wore away against
without peace,
I see my years assembling
for the present struggle.
Finally making sense of what was lost,
I put a name on the future
because I belong to myself now,
I'm the root of what I believe,
not what I was.

Casi bíblica ciudad: Chicago

A CARLOTA, A HORTENSIA

A los trece,
cuando este cuerpo recluso y taciturno
era tiempo apenas pronunciado,
me acerqué
al brillo de las voces de la radio
y divisé una ciudad
que me devolvía la mirada,
una ciudad de puertas abiertas
al vaivén del más desamparado.

En la insaciable emanación
de los años
por la barriada polvorienta,
se fue imponiendo
en la pantalla
aquella terca población,
y con ella fui creciendo
y construyendo otras verdades para mí.
Siempre mis ojos hastiados
despertaban
al horizonte de firmes rascacielos
que se repetían
en ecos de cemento
y tonos de cristal.

18

An Almost Biblical City: Chicago

TO CARLOTA, TO HORTENSIA

At thirteen,
my body secluded and sullen
and time hardly noticeable,
I drew near
the bright voices on the radio
and descried a city
that changed the way I looked at things,
a city whose doors were open
to the most forsaken.

In the years's
insatiable effluvium
through the dusty neighborhood,
that stubborn town
dominated the screen,
and constructing alternate truths for myself,
I grew up with it.
Always disgusted, my eyes
woke up
to a hard skyscraper horizon
repeated
in cement echoes
and glass tones.

Chicago for nim is a refuge

Language in the whole volume is his safety net

↳ words

Finales de los 50,
y palabras y palabras fueron llenando
mis zonas de orfandad,
le inventé otra vida
a la vida: yo era el niño
desdoblado por la paradoja
de dormir en casa y de vivir
igual que un amante anónimo
en la casi bíblica ciudad
que con fuerza real hablaba
en muchas lenguas.
Y daba gusto pronunciar su nombre,
extender el mapa
y buscarla muchas veces junto al lago
cubierta de luz y de razón.

Desde mi aldea del sur
y desde entonces,
para alzar este edificio
de convocadas palabras
he venido reptando polvorosamente
desde el hondo tiempo transcurrido,
izando exactamente la esperanza,
sintiéndome más hombre
en las horas de albedrío
por cada bulevar.

The '50s ending
and words and more words
filling up my zones of orphanhood,
I invented a life
different from the one I had: I the child
developed by the paradox
of sleeping at home and living
like an anonymous lover
in the almost biblical city
that grandly spoke with power
in many languages.
And it felt good to say its name,
to unfold the map
and look for it again and again next to the lake
covered with light and meaning.

From my little village in the South
back then
I've come crawling dustily
from the deep time past
to raise this building
made of words I've summoned,
assiduously hauling up hope,
feeling myself more a man
each truly free hour I spend
out on the boulevards.

Convocación de palabras

Yo no era mío todavía.
Era 1960...
y lo recuerdo bien
porque equivocaba a diario
el sentido de los párrafos;
en la umbría de una tarde
enmugrecida con aire desvalido
asistía a la vergüenza
de no entender del todo
lo que el televisor
estaba resonando en blanquinegro.
Desharás, me dije,
las sanciones en tu contra.
Irresoluto adolescente,
recién graduado
y tardío para todo,
disciplinado a no aprender nada,
harás por ti
lo que no pudo el salón de clase.
Ésta será tu fe:

Infraction
bedlam
ambiguous.

Convocation of Words

I still wasn't free.
It was 1960 . . .
and I remember it well
because every day I got the sense
of the paragraphs mixed up;
in the shade of a grimy,
stale-aired afternoon
I felt ashamed
for not understanding
everything the TV set was chattering
in black and white.
You'll undo, I told myself,
all sanctions against you.
Indecisive adolescent,
just graduated
and habitually late,
taught to learn nothing,
you will do for yourself
what the classroom couldn't.
This will be your faith:

Infraction
bedlam
ambiguous.

Las convoqué
en el altar de mi deseo,
llevándolas por necesidad
a la memoria.
En la fecundidad de un instante
me fui multiplicando:
affable
prerogative
egregious.
Cada vez tras otra
asimilé su historia,
lo que equivale a rescatar
lo que era mío:
priggish
eschew
impecunious.
Porque las hice doctrina
repetida horariamente,
de súbito
yo ya no era el mismo de antes:
assiduous
faux pas
suffragette.

Ahora desciendo inagotablemente
de ellas; son
mi hereditaria ofrenda,

I summoned them
at the altar of my desire, → *fervent*
raising them by necessity *desire to fulfill,*
into memory. *to cumplir*
In the fertility of a moment
I was multiplying myself:
affable
prerogative *own ability to*
egregious. *escape from the*
One after another *shadow! shadow,*
I made their history mine,
which was equivalent to redeeming
what was mine: *a repeated*
priggish *doctrine, hasta que*
eschew *se cumple*
impecunious.
Because I turned them
into hourly repeated doctrine,
suddenly
I was not the same as before:
assiduous
faux pas
suffragette.

I descend from them
inexhaustibly now, and they
are my hereditary offering,

huellas de sangre vivida
sobre el papel constante:
exhume
querimonious
kibitzer.

Tenaz oficio
el de crearme en mi propia imagen
cada vez con cada una al pronunciarla:
postprandial
subsequently
y de escribir por fin con voluntad
las catorce letras de mi nombre
y por encima
la palabra
libertad.

moment that he discovers himself

Simbólico.

trails of living blood
on the ever-present paper:
exhume
querimonious
kibitzer.

A constant effort,
creating myself in my own image
each time I pronounced one of them:
postprandial
subsequently
and finally willing myself to write
the fourteen letters of my name
and over them
the word
libertad.

El mandado

Puse la integridad total en la vereda,
y era yo el único que caminaba
en el crepúsculo,
atravesando diagonalmente por el gran
patio de la escuela contigua
en dirección al lugar de los comestibles
a la mitad de la otra cuadra,
cuando no sé qué furia rígida y caliente
se me entrañó con un golpazo
en el estómago,
luego un vacío acídico y de prisa
se me extendió
como un *pinche animal* devoradoramente
revulsivo que se me fue subiendo
en una sucesión de quejidos,
atragantándoseme la ira
sin poder contener la quieta efusión
mojada que me empañó la vida,
vaciar el asedio de la sangre
que se volvió torrente sin salida,
clamor terrible en mi sendero.

Por un instante anduve a tientas.
No hubo refugio bajo la media luz

The Errand

I staked total integrity in the path,
and I was the only one traveling
by twilight,
crossing through
the nearby school's big courtyard
toward the grocery store
a half-block farther down,
when I don't know what rigid hot fury
pounded me
in the stomach,
then next an acid emptiness,
and it spread through me fast
like a ravenously revulsive   } Image
goddamn animal rising up in me
in a series of moans,
choking off my rage
but unable to check
the steady, wet effusion soiling my life,
or end the siege of blood
rushing torrentially toward a dead end,
the clamor terrible in my path.

For awhile I wandered hesitantly.
I had no refuge under the sky's

• dispair

• The images lead us to his pain

del cielo. (¿Quién me mandó por el
entorno de la abdicación, por el
borde de la historia equivocada,
de qué me sirvió la inculcada paz
dominical de las banquillas?)
Quise arrancarme letra por letra
mi nombre, y de repente pude
verme desde fuera, y era igual
que si el error de estar vivo del prójimo
también se midiera
por el andar de mi cuerpo
en aquel atardecer de octubre del 57.

Pero todo fue fugaz que para cuando
arribé a la esquina del solar
se me había pasado la violencia.
Crucé la calle,
abrí la puerta con campanas,
compré las costumbres del pan blanco,
del cuarto de leche, las tortillas.

Y cuando volví contra las sombras
a la hora incierta (sin comprender y
comprendiendo), volví como quien vuelve
desde lejos tras heredar una derrota.
A qué distancia no estaría de mí mismo
que ni cuenta me di que había ingresado

} anger

30

The poem is about / sharing a moment of dispair
· Rage: how helpless he felt.
   and still feels

half-light. (Who ordered me through
abdication's closure, past
the border of bad history,
and why were they drumming peace at me
each Sunday in the pews?)
I wanted to root my name out
letter by letter, and suddenly I could
see myself from the outside,
just as if my neighbor's error of living
was also measured
by my body's wandering
that late October afternoon of '57.

But everything was so fleeting that when
I arrived at the corner of the lot
my feeling of violence had passed.
I crossed the street,
opened the belled door,
bought the usual order of white bread,
a quart of milk, and tortillas.

The rage had passed but he was still wounded

And when I returned against the shadows
at the uncertain hour (without understanding
yet understanding), I returned like someone returning
from afar after suffering defeat.
I must have been so distant from myself
I didn't realize I had gone in

31

· existential poem, a moment that is remembered
↳ confront the past, preserve give it meaning

por la puerta del tiempo doméstico.
Unas manos solícitas (no sé de quién
todavía) me arrimaron la etnicidad del
alimento. Lo demás fue silencio,
y por largos días toda la vida siguió
cabiendo en aquel hondón de nada
hondamente verdadero.

through the door of domestic time.
Some solicitous hands (I still don't know
whose) put food's ethnicity
near me. The rest was silence,
and through long days all life flowed
into that deeply real
depth of nothingness.

- The rage subsides but there's no hope.

- Deeply confessional poetry.

Tú, por si no otro

Pon la voz
donde tengas la memoria,
hombre, que transformaste
la congoja en conciencia
saludable.
Defiende con palabras
cuanto entiendas,
tú, que tragaste el polvo
de las tardes.
Tú, por si no otro,
condenarás desde tu lengua
la erosión de cada contratiempo.

[handwritten: • hablando consigo mismo]

Tú, que viste crecer
los simulacros del hastío,
entenderás cómo el tiempo
consume al indigente;
tú, que te diste
tus propios mandamientos,
sabrás mejor que nadie
por qué les diste la espalda
a los más tenaces muros de tu aldea.

[handwritten: • He takes the anger, the poverty, the discrimination To somehow move him]

You, If No One Else

                    Listen, you
who transformed your anguish
into healthy awareness,
put your voice
where your memory is.
You who swallowed
the afternoon dust,
defend everything you understand
with words.
You, if no one else,
will condemn with your tongue
the erosion each disappointment brings.

You, who saw the images
of disgust growing,
will understand how time
devours the destitute;
you, who gave yourself
your own commandments,
know better than anyone
why you turned your back
on your town's toughest limits.

> • allowing the memory to
> motivate him

> • giving others the tools that
> helped him

No calles,
no eches al olvido
la verdad más persistente,
como hará, tal vez,
el más convencido de los prójimos.
Recuerda bien
la rotación de tus días: la nublazón,
y el lodazal tan fácil
después de una llovizna;
las precarias ventanas que el viento
intermitentemente aventaba
en el invierno, y aquella
habitación de tablas sin calor
donde el frío en tus ropas
buscaba refugiarse.

Di cómo pudiste llegar
hasta aquí, desatrancar
las puertas de la Historia
para ver tus años iniciales,
tu pueblo, los otros.
Di para qué te ha servido
el sereno duende de la rebeldía,
y cómo fuiste
desaprendiendo las lecciones
de aquel maestro, profanador omnipotente
de tu patria.

do not accept this, speak up, change is your hand

Don't hush,
don't throw away
the most persistent truth,
as our hard-headed brethren
sometimes do.
Remember well
what your life was like: cloudiness,
and slick mud
after a drizzle;
flimsy windows the wind
kept rattling
in winter, and that
unheated slab dwelling
where coldness crawled
up in your clothes.

Tell how you were able to come
to this point, to unbar
History's doors
to see your early years,
your people, the others.
Name the way
rebellion's calm spirit has served you,
and how you came
to unlearn the lessons
of that teacher,
your land's omnipotent defiler.

•Turningpoint, changing

• He wants to inspire anyone

Haz memoria
de cómo te fuiste salvando
desde el primer vacío,
y pregúntate para qué,

después de todo,

pueden servir estas palabras
en esta rotunda hora del presente
donde tu voz suena con tiempo.

Remember how,
from the first emptiness,
you started saving yourself,
and ask yourself what,

after all,

these words are good for
in this round hour now
where your voice strikes time.

Cuento del cronista

He dicho,
por ejemplo: umbral, memoria, cerrazón,
zonas de orfandad, silencio, respirar.
El secreto, sin embargo,
está en habitar otras palabras,
en verlo todo a un tiempo y me desvelo.

Vigila por mí, Tlacuilo venerable,

ayúdame a ser fiel a mi linaje, las fechas
castigadas por el sol y lavadas por la sombra.
Bendíceme, dile a tus dioses que oren por mí.
Prefiero no olvidar
la sucesión de sueños rotos, pues sería
igual que querer quemar la historia.
Instrúyeme, escribano y dibujante,
dame luz y poderío a fin de rescatar
las ruinas de la patria y el orden natural
del tiempo derrumbado.
Dale a mis retablos equilibrio,

Chronicler's Story

                                                  I've said,
for example: threshold, memory, storm threat,
zones of orphanhood, silence, breathing.
The secret, however, is
to inhabit other words
while seeing everything at once and staying awake.

Watch over me, venerable Tlacuilo,

help me be faithful to my heritage, the times
scourged by the sun and washed by shade.
Bless me, tell your gods to pray for me.
I don't want to forget
the succession of broken dreams—that would be
the same as wanting to burn history down.
Scribe and artist, teach me,
give me light and power to restore
the ruins of the land and the natural order
of broken time.
Give my retrospective tableaux balance,

• mainstream history and his own history

• 2 cultures that play in the poem: Indigena and
Castellana.

la medida igual de los colores más constantes
para que ardan de verdad.

Tú también, desflechado peregrino castellano,
Álvar Núñez Cabeza de Vaca, maldito explorador
de nombre imaginista,
enséñame a entender el alfabeto ahora
y por encima de estas huellas ofrecidas.
Enséñame a salvarme de aquéllos que con
mano airada separaron la esperanza germinal
de mi inicial suspiro e hicieron los días naufragar.
Casi-indígena bilingüe por la vertiente
de Texaztlán a la deriva, haz que las aguas
de un río que vadeaste batan mi memoria,
que mi tierra resuene letra a letra debajo
de mi puño, pues es severa y desesperadamente
preciso recitar estas costumbres.

Me pongo a pensar y digo: Ayer es viejo
como un nombre que no deja de decir su historia.
Tlacuilo, Núñez Cabeza de Vaca,
conmigo estáis reconciliados oyendo
esta impaciencia, este diario acto de vivir.

• He calls on the spirits of the Aztecwarrior
and the spanish Conqueror

42

the same intensity the truest colors have,
so they'll be on fire with truth.

You, too, Álvar Núñez Cabeza de Vaca,
disoriented Castilian wanderer,
curst explorer with the imagistic name,
teach me to understand the alphabet now
beyond these proffered impressions.
Teach me to save myself from those who
with wrathful hand cut off the germinal hope
from my first breath on and wrecked my days.
You, almost natively bilingual,
flowing in the drift across Texaztlán,
make the waters of a river you forded beat
against my memory so my land will resound
letter by letter beneath my fist, so my recitation
of these customs will be severely, desperately precise.

I set about thinking and say: yesterday's old,
like a name that doesn't stop telling its history.
Tlacuilo, Núñez Cabeza de Vaca,
hearing this impatience, this daily act of living,
you are reconciled in me.

El angosto marco de mi tiempo

Sintiéndome gastado por el vil → cansado
aburrimiento, y sin saber todavía
cómo borrar en cada paso una barrera,
pisé el umbral temible
y me encontré de súbito perdido
entre los muebles familiares
y oscuridad indivisible de mi alcoba.
En aquella noche insomne,
—marzo tibio del 58—
tirado bocarriba entre el ensueño
y la vigilia, preguntándome
quién más quién menos avanzaba
entre su pueblo,
comprendí con mis huesos más que nunca
el angosto marco de mi tiempo.
Tendrás que irte de aquí me dije.
Haz como puedas para alzarte a otro
estado donde no tengas que entregarte
dócil a la patria.

En el espejo del recuerdo
aún me veo
en aquel nocturno enclaustramiento
sin ninguna herencia de verdad

como Sandra Cisneros

Don't be subssive to other's plans for you, do what you can for a better life

• represents a milestone in his life

44

• he had to embrace his history, his difficulties
To be able to move on

7

My Narrow Frame of Time

Feeling myself worn out by vile
tediousness, and still not knowing
how to obliterate a barrier with each step,
I crossed the terrible threshold
and suddenly met myself lost
among the familiar furniture
and indivisible gloominess of my bedroom.
During that sleepless,
warm March night of '58,
flung mouth up between fantasy
and vigil, asking myself
who more, who less was advancing
in his town,
more than ever I understood in my bones
my narrow frame of time.
You'll have to leave here, I told myself.
Do what you can to raise yourself to another
state where you don't have to give in,
making yourself docile to the land.

In the mirror of memory
I still see myself
in that cloistered night
with no heritage of truth

* Don't be submisse

a que atenerme: cerré los ojos y me metí
a las aguas tenebrosas del cansancio,
y así me fui a contrarrío
hasta la fuente más cálida del sueño.

to depend on: I shut my eyes and going under
the dark waters of fatigue
swam countercurrent
toward the warmest source of sleep.

Entreactos de ira

Reunido está en la remembranza
aquel hogar hermético,
y en él una familia
tan dada a las riñas repentinas
por no tener lo suficiente
para evitarlas.
Estoy oyendo
dos décadas de unos
contra otros: abuelo y tíos
defendiéndose con voces
que hacían doler las paredes
de yeso y de cartón; mayores
contra menores vociferándose
injurias sin ir más allá de la protesta
como quienes se dicen protestantes.
Y daba lástima que sus cuerpos
ya no se llamasen por sus nombres
y que el respeto
se perdiese en el hostil estrépito
de la argumentación.
Lejos de todo dios, era igual
que si dejasen de ser
los elegidos de la tierra,
rendidores de alabanzas

• a lot of fighing, loud

48

• In church was one way, at home was totally ≠

Angry Entr'actes

That hermetic home
comes back together in memory,
and in it a family
prone to sudden quarrels
because they don't have what it takes
to avoid them.
I'm hearing
two decades of them
going at each other: grandfather and uncles
defending themselves with voices
that made the plaster
and cardboard walls hurt; older
against younger, shouting insults
without going further than the protest,
like those called Protestants.
And it was pitiful their bodies
weren't called anymore by their names
and respect
was lost in the hostile crash
of argument.
So far from God, it was as if
they had stopped being
the chosen of the earth,
the devout full of praises

• Trying to get away from his house

• Young man's confusion

en fervor dominical.
Perdonadme, madre absoluta,
abuelo y tíos de la vida, pues
nunca comprendí por qué éramos
mejor que el vecino y los "paganos",
y mucho menos
cuál era la lección
que me querían enseñar.

~

En aquellos entreactos de ira
nada hacía prever alguna redención.
Huía hacia mí mismo; me hacía sordo
para salvar lo que pudiese
tras cada huamazo de humillación.
Del rincón aparte (a donde nadie
venía por mí) me agarraba,
y en la garganta estaba el golpe
de todos los resabios.
De repente alguien perdía,
y con lágrimas
lavaba el resto de su noche.
Sólo así cesaba
el aire intransigente.
Y calmados alma y cuerpo,
una tregua inquietantemente silenciosa
invadía cada habitación.

in Sunday fervor.
Pardon me, imperious mother,
grandfather and aunts and uncles,
I never understood why we were
better than the neighbors and the "pagans,"
much less
what the lesson was
you wanted to teach me.

he felt totally disconnected

~

I couldn't see any redemption
coming from those angry entr'actes.
I escaped into myself, I made myself deaf
to save what I could
after each humiliating blow.
From my place apart (where no one
came for me) I held on,
and the pain from all
the viciousness was in my throat.
Suddenly someone lost
and washed
the rest of the night with tears.
Only in that way
did the feeling of horror stop.
And soul and body calmed,
an uneasily silent truce
invading each room.

• More into his private space

• Disturbance in his life was not only external, but also internal, coming from his family

~

Porque soy yo y mi conciencia
vuelvo hacia atrás y me miro
donde estoy.
Es domingo, noviembre del 81,
y si hoy
a los míos enjuicio a mi manera,
no es porque quisiese tener razón,
sino sólo porque he sobrevivido
para entender:
que el monedero
vacío ante la vida;
que el hedor de la letrina de madera
donde las moscas luminosamente
rezumbaban verdeoscuras alrededor
de los montículos comunalmente putrefactos;
que el cuerpo
doblado a campo abierto
para arrancar el fruto de otros;
que el agua que tardaba en calentarse
sobre la leña para lavarse
los lesivos días llevados a la espalda;
y que la escasa volición
por traspasar los cercados
de la maldición,
     fueron dejando
sus huellas en aquellos seres

~

Because I am I and my awareness
I go back and look at myself
where I am.
It's Sunday, November '81,
and if today
I pass judgment on my own in my own way,
it's not because I want to be right,
but only because I've survived
in order to understand:
life
with an empty pocketbook,
the outhouse stench
where the luminous dark-green flies
buzzed around
the mounds rotting communally,
the body
stooped over in the open field
to pick other people's food,
the water on the open fire that took a long time
to get hot enough to wash away
the wounding days hauled on the back,
and the meager will
to go beyond the limits
of damnation—
　　they were leaving
their marks on the creatures

de tierra y de sudor,
   y eran en el fondo
las abyectas referencias
que hacían gritar con desamor.

~

En fin, ya, gracias a la vida
por la memoria insosegada
que es memoria.
Diez años, quince,
muchos días pasarían
para trazar los rumbos de esta génesis,
para encontrar estos versículos
del libre respirar.

of dirt and sweat
    and were in essence
the reasons why, feeling so abject,
they cried out in hate.

~

Finally, now, I give life thanks ⌉
for the unappeased memory   ⎬
that is memory.   ⌟
Ten years, fifteen,
a long time had to pass
for me to sketch out the routes of this genesis,
for me to find these versicles ⌉
of a free man breathing.   ⎬

La aventuranza de la sedición

El sol irrestricto
había partido el día en dos,
y ahora íbamos
en el filo de la tarde
igual que un retablo de corvas
figuras de lona azul distante.
Íbamos como una peregrina
y maloliente hermandad de sudores,
tirón a tirón entre las matas
de algodón frondoso,
con la patética ilusión de llegar
al final del surco.
Mas siempre que arribábamos
con la prisa de la necesidad de estar ahí,
la única lógica era
que nos tocaba devolvernos
por el surco contrario,
cuya opuesta continuidad
nadie podía represar.

Y yo, el niño polvoriento
quedado atrás a la mitad de la labor,
detenido en el remanso de mi sombra,
tenía razón

The Venturesomeness of Sedition

The unrestricted sun
had split the day in two,
and now we went
on the edge of the afternoon
like a tableau of bent figures
made of faded blue duck.
We went like a wandering
and stinking, sweating brotherhood,
pull by pull between ⌐
the leafy cotton plants, ⌡
with the pathetic appearance of arriving
at the end of the furrow.
But we always arrived
in a rush to get there,
and the sole logic was
we had to move over
to the next furrow,
and no one could stop
the counterflow down it.

And I, the dusty kid
left behind in the middle of the field,
held prisoner in my own slow shadow,
was right

en no darle vida a los pasos absurdos
por herencia.
Y así se fueron quemando los días
en aquella estación cautiva
de la infancia.

Entonces sería,
sí, sería entonces que me entró
la aventuranza de la sedición.
Los sábados,
pasado el mediodía,
acostaba, por fin, el cuerpo
a las orillas del baño de aluminio.
Y en el rito liberador del agua,
podía quitarme de encima
la costra y contemplar
las aguas turbias del tiempo.
Y así fue,
con la ablución del baño semanal,
que cada vez me fui
desterrando de lo que era.

in not giving in to the absurd pace
of tradition.
So my days burned up
in that captive state
of childhood.

Then, yes,
it was then the venturesomeness
of sedition overtook me.
Saturdays,
after noon,
the body finally lying down
in the waves of the aluminum bathtub.
And in the liberating rite of the water,
I could shed
the grime and contemplate
the muddy waters of time.
So it was,
with the ablution of the weekly bath,
I exiled myself each time
from what I was.

Tierras prometidas

Era fácil no despertar
tan de mañana,
pero ya por el entresueño de la casa
entraban y salían
figuras desteñidas
acarreando no sé qué cajas
como por sumisión a un itinerario.
Cómo olvidar que el desayuno
lo tomaba sin estar consciente,
que de pronto sonaba el metal
contra el metal
al engancharse una *treila* verde
de dos ruedas,
cargadora de bultos
de doméstica intención.

Ahora todos los viajes
son uno: a buena hora
y bien dispuestos salíamos
por la carretera de chicle
abandonada
(recuerdo siempre un carro negro),
salíamos furtivamente
mucho antes de la media luz,

Promised Lands

Many a morning
it was easy not to wake up,
but already discolored figures
were entering and leaving
through the half-dreamt house
carrying I don't know what kind of boxes
as if they were on a timetable.
How can I forget eating breakfast
without being aware of it,
or how suddenly metal rang
against metal
as a green two-wheeled trailer
was hooked up
to haul bundles
of household goods.

Now all the journeys
are one: very early
and hopeful, we left
by the empty
asphalt highway
(I always remember a black car),
we left secretly,
well before first light,

como quienes deseaban
ahorrarse la vergüenza de vivir.
Y daban ganas de no ir, de descansar
de las veces anteriores.
Cada verano retoñábamos
porque la tierra hacia el sur
(El Campo, Wharton, Taiton,
New Taiton, Glen Flora)
prometía capullos y verdor;
porque no había modo
de aliviar la vida de esa vida,
de redimirnos
de una sola tarde excesivamente
soleada cuando el cuerpo
se enjuagaba en el sudor,
y las dagas del sol
nos traicionaban por la espalda.
(¿Quién vendrá por mí un día
a curarme del horror de estar aquí,
a quitarme la sed para siempre
y por favor?)

~

Muy entrado septiembre
y ya rendidas las plantas
yo seguía siendo el niño involuntario,
pues no había otra esperanza

like people who wanted
to be spared the shame of living.
And I felt like not going, like resting
from earlier times.
Each summer we reappeared
because the land toward the south
(El Campo, Wharton, Taiton,
New Taiton, Glen Flora)
promised cotton bolls and green fields;
because there was no way
to lighten that life's life,
to redeem us
from one single excessively sunny
afternoon when the body
was soaked with sweat,
and the sun's daggers
let us have it in the back.
(Please, who will come one day for me
to cure me of the horror
of being here, to quench
my thirst forever?)

~

Far on into September,
the plants already dried up,
I continued being the indolent child,
because I had no other hope

más que la de subirnos
al camino hacia el norte
(Hale Center, Plainview,
Levelland, Seymour, Seminole)
donde repentinamente ya estábamos
atragantándonos con la arena fría,
donde otra vez íbamos a contrarreloj
codo a codo
como una jorobada masa congénita
por el estado repartida
            arropados
agachados   ahincados
por encima de la helada quebradiza
marcados por el rozón del ramaje,
dando el preciso tirón y arrancón
a capullos con cáscara seca.
Íbamos por el mes de enero,
y un vientecillo nos odiaba
cada vez que levantábamos la cara.
Allí también sólo los terrones,
no la tierra, eran nuestros.
(Quién fuera liebre para dar
el salto vital, para correr,
correr de aquí y no volver.)

Desde toda la sustancia
que hoy me pertenece,

than for us to go
north up the road
(Hale Center, Plainview,
Levelland, Seymour, Seminole)
where suddenly we were already
choking with the cold sand,
where we were racing the clock again
elbow to elbow
like a congenitally humpbacked mass
spread out through the state
                wrapped up
stooped over   kneeling
through the brittle frost
and scratched by the scythelike stalks
as we gave the necessary pull and snap
to dry-hulled bolls.
We went through the month of January,
and a light wind bit us
each time we lifted our faces.
There also only the clods
were ours, not the land.
(I wished I were a jackrabbit so I could make
the great leap, to run,
to run away and not come back.)

Because of all
I'm concerned with today,

con más razón ahora considero,
cuán presa estuvo aquella infancia
en el dominio aborrecible
de las labores de algodón.
¿Quién mandó que en los 40
fueran tan largos los surcos,
y que el tiempo
que tardé en piscarlos
fuera voraz para mi vida?
En los 50 ya no me importaba
la respuesta. Me dije:
todo está perdido, andavete
como puedas. De aquí no sacas nada.
Mas sólo en los 60 pude separar
el pasado del futuro,
y dejar atrás los caminos de la malasombra
y de la escarcha.

I give more thought now
to how prisonlike that childhood was
in the abhorrent world
of cotton-field work.
Who gave the order in the '40s
the furrows had to be so long,
and the time
that dragged in picking them
should slaver to devour me?
In the '50s the answer
was already unimportant to me. I told myself:
everything's lost, get up and go
as best you can. You're not getting anything here.
I couldn't separate past from future
till the '60s,
and leave the hot unshaded roads behind,
and the ones frozen over.

Ahora somos cuerpo y tiempo

Si algo he dicho
más allá
de las deshonras
de la infancia;
si algo he sido
más allá
de la descarga del *desmadre*
y de las sombras insolentes,
será porque uno de entre tantos
desde el resol de los 60
un día dijo una palabra.
Se la dijo a nadie.
Se la dijo a todos
y alianzas se formaron en el aire,
y ya todo fue distinto.
De esta forma el hombre
que mejor conozco
cobró dureza y temple,
y yo también
pacté con los nuevos actos
de los hombres y mujeres
del espejo y de la luz.

Ahora somos cuerpo y tiempo,
porque es el peso transparente

We're Substance Now and Time

If I have spoken about something
beyond
the violations
of childhood,
if I have been something
more than
one of the *wretched*
unloading his insolent shadows,
it's likely because out of the sun's glare
of the '60s one among many
said a word one day.
He said it to no one.
He said it to everyone
and everything came together,
then everything was different.
In this way the man
I know best
gained sharpness and courage,
and I also
made a covenant with the new acts
of the men and women
of mirrors and light.

We're substance now and time,
because it's the transparent weight

del nosotros,
y no la Historia por sí sola
lo que marca
otra dirección del aire,
otros caminos.

of ourselves,
and not History by itself alone
that marks
a different direction of the air,
different roads.

Unción de palabras

¿Qué dirán mañana estas palabras,
qué dirán
entre las manos de los hijos
de este padre que aún no lo es?
¿Verán
que he interrumpido la vida
para contar estas constancias,
estos retazos de lamento,
y que he venido con los míos
de un pueblo perseguido
por la historia irracional?
¿Comprenderán
que este fragor de consonantes
es el asco
en conciencia transformado,
cabal comprobación de que he existido?

Llévate, hija,
llévate, hijo,
de mí esta unción de palabras
con las que me curo diariamente,
porque el recuerdo es poderoso
y se vuelve contra mí al improviso,
tiene vida como tú,

Anointing by Words

What will these words say tomorrow,
what will they say
to the children of this father
who's still not a father?
Will they see
I have interrupted my life
to relate these records,
these sorrow-filled fragments,
that I have come with my own
from a people
persecuted by senseless history?
Will they understand
this clamor of rimes
is disgust
transformed into awareness,
thorough proof I've existed?

Take on yourself, daughter,
take on yourself, son,
this anointing by words
I recover daily by,
because memory is powerful
and suddenly turns against me
and has life just as you do,

aunque todavía no existes,
y sin embargo, dulcemente,
ya de ti hago memoria.

Hoy me desamarro
del trágico trasunto de la vida,
y te entrego, pues,
las cosas familiares: cómo
y por qué una mitad de tus abuelos,
más quien esto escribe,
tardamos largamente en despedirnos
de la vecindad donde dolían
nuestros nombres.

Para siempre:
llévate esta fe enmarcada
a fin de que retengas el retrato
y tu linaje
inquietados en el fondo
por las fracturas del pasado
y la entereza que ya soy.

although you don't exist yet,
nevertheless, sweetly now,
I already remember you.

Today I unbind myself
from the tragic sense of life
and deliver to you
the familiar things: how
and why half your ancestors,
plus the one writing this,
have been so late quitting
the neighborhood where our names
gave grief.

Forever:
take this faith I've framed
so you can keep this picture
and your lineage
restless in the background
with the breaks in the past
and the wholeness I've attained.

Notas

"Clase de historia"
Las citas en inglés se extraen del libro de John C. Duval, *The Adventures of Big-Foot Wallace, the Texas Ranger and Hunter*, del cual les leía a sus alumnos un cierto maestro de historia en la escuela secundaria en la década de los 50.

"Convocación de palabras"
Las voces inglesas intercaladas han sido extraídas del gran acervo de vocabulario que el autor almacenó en unas libretas entre los años 1960 y 1964 durante un período de consciente autodidactismo, lo cual le resultó ser un no insignificante primer paso hacia la universidad si bien entonces lo ignorase.

"El mandado"
pinche animal, alusión al *angst* existencial del cual padece el protagonista del relato, "The Week of the Life of Manuel Hernández", por Nick Vaca.

"Cuento del cronista"
Los Tlacuilos eran escribanos aztecas que cumplían la tarea de cronistas encargados de los códices. *Texaztlán*, neologismo compuesto de *Texas*, estado en el sudoeste de los EUA, y *Aztlán*, voz náhuatl que se refiere a la "tierra hacia el norte", o sea el territorio mítico de los aztecas supuestamente ubicado en el sudoeste de la Unión norteamericana. Según Rémi Siméon, Aztlán es el "lugar ocupado por los aztecas en sus orígenes, cuyo emplazamiento, objeto de numerosas búsquedas, sigue ignorado. Generalmente se le localiza al norte del golfo de California" (*Diccionario de la lengua náhuatl o mexicana* [Paris: Imprimérie Nationale, 1885; México: edición Siglo Veintiuno, 1981], p. 51).

"Ahora somos cuerpo y tiempo"
desmadre, privación en la vida social, alienación y derrotismo, o bien tragedia del espíritu. Los versos en cursiva se toman del ensayo de Octavio Romano, "Goodbye Revolution—Hello Slum". Traducción de quien escribe.

Notes

"History Class"
The citations in English are taken from John C. Duval, *The Adventures of Big-Foot Wallace, the Texas Ranger and Hunter*, which a certain high school history teacher read to his pupils in the '50s.

"Convocation of Words"
The interpolated words in English have been taken from the big supply of vocabulary words the author stored in notebooks between 1960 and 1964, during a period of conscientious self-teaching, which ended up being a not-so-insignificant first step to the university, though he did not know it then.

"The Errand"
pinche animal (goddamn animal), allusion to the existential angst suffered by the protagonist of the short story "The Week of the Life of Manuel Hernández" by Nick Vaca.

"Chronicler's Story"
The Tlacuilos were Aztec scribes who worked as chroniclers in charge of the codices. *Texaztlán*, a neologism composed of *Texas* and *Aztlán*, the latter a Náhuatl word that refers to the "land to the north" that is the mythical territory of the Aztecs supposedly situated in the Southwest of the United States. According to Rémi Siméon, Aztlán is the "place occupied by the Aztecs in their beginnings, whose location, the object of numerous searches, remains unknown. Generally it is situated north of the Gulf of California" (*Diccionario de la lengua náhuatl o mexicana* [Paris: Imprimérie Nationale, 1885; México: Siglo Veintiuno, 1981], p. 51).

"We're Substance Now and Time"
desmadre, deprivation in social life, alienation and defeatism, or tragedy of spirit. The lines in italics were taken from an essay by Octavio Romano, "Goodbye Revolution—Hello Slum." Translation by the writer.

Translator's Afterword

The unforced elegance in Tino Villanueva's poetry evokes a comfortable sense of dignity. Qualified by reportorial incisiveness and emotional bite, a contemplative attitude has increasingly informed his work. It was there in *Hay Otra Voz Poems* (1972) and *Shaking Off the Dark* (1984); it is even more prominent in his subsequent collection, *Crónica de mis años peores* (1987), in which he turned to a sustained meditation on his childhood years growing up with migratory farmworkers in Texas during the 1940s and '50s. More than confessional, his accounts are emblematic of a major portion of the American psyche that, whatever the ethnic point of reference, has traditionally been associated with the promise of energy and the pain of estrangement.

Because of the striking presence of both lyricism and will in his work, Villanueva's voice is markedly different from that of many of his contemporaries who, loyal to the oddly tyrannical demands of plainspeech, often write arhythmic, monotonal verse. Plainspeech poetry can certainly be interesting, even rich, tonally as well as informationally, if the subject matter is right; but unfortunately the plainspeech phenomenon has become in our day little more than mannerism, a workshoplike withdrawal from the demands and possibilities of vision and eloquence. Absence of adornment can suggest stylistic integrity, an elegantly songlike economy even, but it can also indicate dullness, an absence of intensity.

Consistent with his North American identity, Villanueva presents his reflections obliquely as often as directly. Incidents become metaphors, and metaphors become modes of perception that keep two points of perspective in harmony. As a result, the poems in *Chronicle of My Worst Years* are neither soft with nostalgia nor hysterical with bitterness. They portray a rigorous sense of detachment with an intense subjectivity, and that duple effect is consistent with the ancient concept of prophetic poet, a figure who has traditionally functioned simultaneously as outsider and insider.

As he weaves images from the past into coherent shapes, he avoids being locked into motionlessness between the external and internal worlds. Just as he proves that strong passion and sharp insight are not necessarily alien to each other, he also shows that when one operates on the border between worlds as well as on both sides of that border, one does not have to become paralyzed at the junctions where conflicting tensions often meet.

Throughout the reflections in *Chronicle*, Villanueva describes the processes of his self-creation and, in doing so, returns to his first language, Spanish. In previous collections he used both Spanish and English. In addition to meditations on the poverty and anguish associated with his past, pieces in the book convey the harsh particulars associated with following migratory farm jobs through extreme heat and cold and encounters with unashamedly bigoted schoolteachers. Having left that world, he says in "History Class" ("Clase de historia"):

> Here my life scars over
> because I'm the deserter,
> the profane impenitent who quit
> the crazy class,
> the insurrectionist
> stripped of the creeds of negation.

> Aquí mi vida cicatriza
> porque soy el desertor,
> el malvado impenitente que ha deshabitado
> el salón de la demencia,
> el insurrecto
> despojado de los credos de la negación.

Under the circumstances, the speaker's assumption of responsibility is startling; but in our time noble gestures often are.

In many respects the process of the collection has a double function. A record of a painful, exhaustingly transient childhood, it is also an analytical treatment of the speaker's artistic drive toward frankness and the possibilities of transcendence. Incisively maintaining his own sense of separateness and its spiritual opposite, compassion, he refuses to be swept up by the self-protecting illusions of clannish pride. As he says in "Angry Entr'actes" ("Entreactos de ira"):

> I never understood why we were
> better than the neighbors and the "pagans,"

> nunca comprendí por qué éramos
> mejor que el vecino y los "paganos",

His sense of separateness, along with an inclusiveness of attitude, ensures the maintenance of balanced perspective. In fact, he may be one of the few poets in the United States who has not given up on wisdom as a possible consequence of understanding. He does admit, however, that his hold on endurance was sometimes tentative:

> a long time had to pass
> for me to sketch out the routes of this genesis,

for me to find these versicles
of a free man breathing.

muchos días pasarían
para trazar los rumbos de esta génesis,
para encontrar estos versículos
del libre respirar.

Throughout the work, idea and fact are presented as parts of
a single complex. Language is seen as the path to freedom,
and the textures of that path have a sacramental quality that
affirms the ritualistically evocative possibilities of speech, or
art as the way to redemption.

Dramatizing his efforts to master English, to expand his
range of knowledge, "Convocation of Words" ("Convo-
cación de palabras") describes Villanueva's process of "multi-
plying" himself by summoning the words he learned "at the
altar of my desire" (en el altar de mi deseo) where "I made
their history mine" (asimilé su historia). Embracing the sacra-
mental possibilities of art in "Anointing by Words" ("Unción
de palabras"), he sees his poetry as a living extension of self:

What will these words say tomorrow,
what will they say
to the children of this father
who's still not a father?

¿Qué dirán mañana estas palabras,
qué dirán
entre las manos de los hijos
de este padre que aún no lo es?

Because he does not submit to the tired notions of alienation
and fragmentation, he seems to be making a breakthrough for
others outside himself when, in "You, If No One Else" ("Tú,

por si no otro"), he admonishes himself to "Put your voice /
where your memory is" (Pon la voz / donde tengas la memo-
ria). It's instructive to note that the result of this self-exami-
nation is neither disillusionment nor hysteria, what in another
poem he rightly calls "the blinding fraud" (fraude cegador),
but transcendence through the compensatory possibilities of
imagination—imagination seen here as force for understand-
ing rather than fantasy. Illustrating the difficult process of
working beyond the chaos of hatred, he remembers a teacher
who read to his Anglo and Hispanic students passages like
"*beware of the Mexicans . . . Put fresh caps on / your revolver
. . . They are a great / deal more treacherous than Indians . . .
And that's one reason I hate them so.*" One winces when
reading of the boy's response:

> To keep from crying out the anger boiling up in me
> I bent over my desk
> like a human question mark;
>
> Por no gritar mi urgente ira,
> me encorvaba en el pupitre
> como un cuerpo interrogante;

The boy imagines himself "in another state" (en otro estado).
"State" (estado), of course, has a double meaning here. Refer-
ring both to place and attitude, it is emblematic of Villanue-
va's concept of language as locus for idea and fact, a matter
subtly different, for example, from that concept of language
merely as a tool for pointing to objects and concepts outside
itself.

A serious presence in contemporary American letters, Vil-
lanueva has a reflective voice of his own. The largeness of
spirit in his poetry rejoins the contemplative narrator with the

textures of his and his people's past. The poems gathered here are not so much notes about impulses to escape pain and horror as they are ritualistic utterances whose litanic effects temper threats of dissemblement into an authentically aesthetic power.

JAMES HOGGARD